The Luck

The Luck is **Jane Routh**'s fifth collection of poetry Smith|Doorstop has published. *Circumnavigation* won the Poetry Business Book and Pamphlet competition in 2002 and was shortlisted for the Forward First Collection Prize; *Teach Yourself Mapmaking* was a PBS Recommendation. Individual poems have won several competitions including the Academi Cardiff International and Strokestown International Competitions, and the Long Poem Prize from Second Light.

Jane lives on the northern edge of the Forest of Bowland, where she looks after Ancient Semi-Natural Woodland and new woods she has planted for the future. Smith|Doorstop also published *Falling into Place*, her prose book about a year's life and work in this area of north Lancashire.

The Luck
Jane Routh

smith|doorstop

the poetry business

Published 2024
by The Poetry Business
Campo House,
54 Campo Lane,
Sheffield S1 2EG
www.poetrybusiness.co.uk

Copyright © Jane Routh 2024
The moral rights of the author have been asserted.
ISBN 978-1-914914-87-4

All rights reserved.
Without limiting the rights under copyright reserved above, no part of this publication may be reproduced, storied in or introduced into a retrieval system, or transmitted, in any form or by any means (electronic, mechanical, photocopying, recording or otherwise), without the prior written permission of both the copyright owner and the above publisher of this book.

Designed & typeset by Utter.
Printed by Imprint Digital

British Library Cataloguing-in-Publication Data.
A catalogue record for this book is available from the British Library.

Smith|Doorstop is a member of Inpress
www.inpressbooks.co.uk.

Distributed by BookSource, 50 Cambuslang Road,
Cambuslang Investment Park, Glasgow G32 8NB.

The Poetry Business gratefully acknowledges the support
of Arts Council England.

Contents

- 9   Out of time
- 10   Viruses
- 13   The verge,
- 14   Walking around
- 15   Walking around II
- 16   The February Museum: recent acquisitions
- 19   The dead never leave
- 20   A wary glance ahead
- 21   Hearthed
- 23   Beam
- 25   The houses
- 26   The dead never leave II
- 27   Shelved
- 29   Spine
- 31   The dead never leave III
- 32   It's called 'Shifting Baseline Syndrome'
- 33   'When a man grows old, he starts to plant trees'
- 34   The dead never leave IV
- 35   Back then
- 36   Knock knock knockin' on morning's door
- 38   The dead never leave V
- 39   Note to self
- 40   Topping and tailing blackcurrants at the back window
- 41   Redlisted
- 43   Dry
- 44   Seen when not looking
- 45   Hold out your hand,
- 46   The sighting
- 48   A short cut home

50	Having the luck
52	Sometimes they recover
53	yesterday the wind
54	Namesake
55	September again
56	Why it's hard to concentrate
58	Album
60	Thirteenth of December
61	Minus 8°C
62	An 'Arctic maritime airmass impact'
63	Second of January
64	The last resort
65	Without which
66	Which way up to chit a potato?
68	Walking Around III
69	*Malus sylvestris*, 60-90 cm, January 2022
70	Tree correspondence (NZ)
72	The Old Wood
73	It's a mast year again
74	Idle talk,
76	Notes
77	Acknowledgements

Out of time

Days have detached themselves from the calendar
repeating like the tick at the end of old 78s
and the weather colludes: the third week of sun
or the fourth? – blossom on wild cherries
against always a background of blue.

My watch has stopped at 15.35. The battery sort. *14th April 2020*
No market. No stallholder who could fix it.
My father gave me my mother's wind-up watch
warning it would be no use: one of those
that would only work on the wrist it knew.

Meantime birch trees relax into green haze –
one long inbreath of catkins, leaves, expansion and seeds
before their outbreath shedding and regathering.
Lambs on the hill slow down and fatten. Ash hold back
but beech shed last year's browns, make ready

– all of that and bluebells and early purples
and going by the light and listening to your body clock
would make it feel like a holiday   but for the thin fog
of anxiety that doesn't disperse and   yes
this   guilt   at any joy   *15th April 2020*
                    Two million confirmed infections worldwide

Viruses

H5N1   2007

Masks, gloves: we've been here before
blindly warding off unknowables
and worrying at 3am about deaths.
The waiting, uncertainty, fear –
but that was then and for the birds:
clamp-down immediate, no movement,
no mixing with the wild and
a cull at any sign of illness.

We said *cull* ourselves, the word
at one remove from *kill*. But that
was then and there were rules
to follow in our boots and rubber gloves:
feed on concrete then hose down,
no visitors, no touching and stay clear
if you have any sort of symptom.

That was for the birds and nevermind
their protests, their wanting life
as and where it always was;
nevermind their threats and hissing,
that rules were there. The virus lost.
The flock survived, two (now ancient)
ganders with us still. I had
a poultry worker's vaccination.

FMDV Type O pan Asia   2001

Lockdown. Dread. No
'wait and see'. No 'possible' scenarios.
Listening at 3am for tyres
through straw and disinfectant
along your road: *Just stay away!*
At any sign, the slaughter:
creatures you birthed, talked with
in some mutual understanding
dumped in lorryloads by JCBs.

Smoke from the pyres and an eerie glow
in the north west skies. Nevermind
mere business gone: it was your life
your home, your family's history.
Numbness.   Suicides.

And that was then and some stayed on
to milk again. The dread returns
at 3am. Some go on but not
the young and strong drafted in
for good money carting corpses,
good money for the clean-up
spraying chemicals but costed now
by cracked and always-peeling skin,
breath hard come by, strength all gone.

SARS-CoV-2   *12 March 2020*

This is now, this waiting
and uncertainty. This fear is new
and for ourselves: the mind at 3am
racing round deranged absurdities:
how old is 'elderly', do some age
sooner, some later than their friends?
Exact locations and exclusion zones
used to keep us up-to-date
for farms with animal disease
but we've no handholds
for being grounded here and now
with so much missing information
of whereabouts and when and   even here?
and keeping safe and how   and what
we'll need   our wits   all   scattered
   and with them   words

The verge,

that passive sweep of rough grass where tractor drivers
pull over – not to let you by but because it's the spot
they pick up a phone signal – has recast itself
after this gussey weather, *overnight* I want to say
at the suddenness of the old hedge throwing up six-foot hazels,
blackthorn roots claiming ground for knee-high spikes
and brambles splayed over, under and across everything,
clusters of red berries already gleaming, the odd black one
if you'd shoulder in through nettles and wade
a thigh-high wild raspberry thicket among hardheads
and tufted vetch and great willow herb,
a patch of palest cream honeysuckle the evening topnote
over damp and rank verdure and crushed fern.

This shock of growth: how can I not have watched it
wilding up this year – it's as if I'd gone missing from my life,
looking away, looking inwards, occupied with human disease,
not even registering when the delivery driver complained
You people, you've no idea how to look after hedges round here.
No one can cut before September, I told him, a man
on the side of vans, not birds, insects, seeds.
We have it all in hand, we think: next month, Kenny
will be along with the flail, tyres flattening the undergrowth
while he squares off the old hedge to an orderly line.
My back turned so briefly and I see
how loose a grip we have on a world on the verge
of turning back to purposes of its own instead of ours.

Walking around

I walk where I always walk: under trees to the road then
wind-at-my back. No traffic. Two cyclists: '... no, level-headed ...',
one other walker, way back. Hedges still uncut:
dusky haws, bright hips, thistledown soggy with dew.

At skid marks where the road narrows, dips, bends,
I cross over, a few strides, cross back where it straightens.
That walker's nearly caught up: footsteps are closing,
loud now, and a voice says 'You know this road well'

so I say 'Home patch' and ask where he's from
(holidaymaker, my guess: new boots, yellow traffic vest).
'Agnes Ing Lane'. He shortens his stride to mine, asks where I live –
knows my footpath well, supposes I'm pretty self-sufficient

and at the junction asks where I'm headed. 'Little Plantation'. He's
going further, 'Fairy Steps'. We're side-by-side uphill and the talk's
all trees: ash die-back and elms we lost in the nineties and
by the corner of the wood we're on to a beech for his birthday

so goodbye. 'Goodbye, enjoy.' 'Goodbye, goodbye.' I jump
into shadow beyond the ditch, wade through male fern and
settle on a birch stump. Maybe he'll have been as glad to recover
his own stride and thoughts as I am to drop back into silence,   solitude.

Walking around II

In the first lockdown, where I always walk
I hesitated: Little Plantation had a squatter.
Hollies are so dense you might not have noticed
if you'd walked in from the top;

if you wandered, as I do, in from the north
you could make out a hammock slung between trunks,
awning and backcloth against weather, bare earth,
rocks round a fire pit, a tarp-covered heap.

It was close to the side of the wood open to fields
and someone had woven a wattle to mask it –
a weekender, camping as a change from lockdown?
No, it had an air of permanence and use

which changed how I walked through the wood, alert
and on edge, re-tuned to the human world.
Sometimes an old white van parked in a gateway
nearby: those times, I didn't walk there.

The February Museum: recent acquisitions

Fraxinus excelsior 18" square-cut deadwood log
with egg galleries of *Hylesinus varius*

>Retrieved from the log pile, a long block
>inscribed with life cycles: straight tunnels
>across the grain where beetles deposited a row of eggs;
>
>along the grain, smaller tunnels widen
>where growing grubs ate their way out into the air.
>Cleaned of frass with a toothpick, pale lines as if drawn
>
>on a dark ground – the way you'd draw Cuthbert's
>ivory comb preserved with him in his coffin,
>fine teeth running out on one side, even more on the other.

Sound recording made on the south side of the Little Wood
of 20mph north-easterly wind gusting 30

>You can hear gusts like a train roaring up and through
>but as if you're on a bridge above a mainline station
>they don't affect you here in the lee of the wood
>
>which shelters downwind for over twenty times
>its own height without eddies or turbulence
>and even upwind slows things down a notch or two
>
>– though it's not much of a wood, only a long strip
>three or four trees deep, bordered by hollies
>hedging what was once a drove road to the moor.

Handful of short hairs cut during a pandemic
from the head of a 78 year old male

> Very fine, very plentiful and dark brown.
> Not even the odd silvery one. No wonder
> the girl in the chemist's checked he was over sixty.
>
> An amateur cut takes four times as long as a barber
> – more, if you count next day's extra snips at tufts
> that were missed, or time picking up hair
>
> all over the kitchen floor and stray bits up sleeves,
> in a pocket, stuck to a jumper – all tossed out
> for birds to line nests with, blown back by the wind.

Silver foil top from glass milk bottle
stamped wording indistinct except for *16*

> If you know what you're looking for,
> you can just make out the *PAST*
> of pasteurised. The bottle it sealed was plain
>
> though you never know what you'll find next
> on the doorstep: an embossed *Cotteslaw Dairies*,
> a painted *Lanchester* and a full-colour Batman
>
> whose blue's worn away – as is the blue of the union flag
> on another – all here after knocking about
> in three dozen fridges before this.

Paterson 500ml perspex darkroom measuring cylinder
graduated in millilitres, 'English' and US fluid ounces

>	Not much used (slightly on the small side
>	for the volume of chemicals needed at 20°C
>	mixed with equal parts water to develop large prints)
>
>	still light in the hand and excessively accurate
>	since now – instead of metol and carbonates and bromide –
>	it measures changes to life and what there is to be measured,
>
>	the darkroom become storeroom and the liquids
>	that need mixing *light (not olive) oil with soya milk*,
>	sometimes tepid water foaming with crumbled yeast.

Annotated February 2021 calendar page
with photograph over Luskentyre towards the Harris hills

>	Many empty squares.
>	Food deliveries on the same day each week.
>	Two birthdays and six online 'events'.
>
>	A bright and windy day over the white shell sands,
>	hills dark in the distance and out west
>	turquoise waves spattered with white crests –
>
>	it always was windy, always cold
>	and the shining expanse of wet sand empty
>	of any sign of what we have done to the world.

The dead never leave

The dead do not leave. On long journeys
or empty roads they settle themselves
into the passenger seat and say
Aren't the hedgerows well-kept; I wonder
who cuts them, repeating themselves
as they always did, Aren't the hedgerows well-kept;
is it the council? They can ask as often as they like,
you're so patient with them now. How well
you are getting to know them, outside
the spotlight of some moment's passing need.

How much better you understand them, not
from the To Whom It May Concern tucked among
old photos, but from seeing them whole. Gone
the contradiction between the younger self
who said they would've gone to college
but for parents who were too poor
and the older self's insistence it was because
they stayed home caring for their father.
You know now that memory's not inventory
but story that retells itself to suit the age.

They follow you everywhere, even into dreams
where everything goes wrong – you know the sort:
they're expecting you, you've no money
and you're at the wrong funeral
and in the crowd you've lost the tall Nigerian
who'd promised a lift in her red Mini
as far as London for the night train north,
so you think you'd better ring them to say
you're on the way – then, wakening,
realise the number that you dialled is your own.

A wary glance ahead

I lean on the rake. Any old ghosts
still haunting the meadow will scoff
at how little of the hay I'm shifting each day.
When I first worked these fields, I wanted
my mother to see the next field downhill,
where you come to the trees at its edge
and the land falls sheer to a river
glittering and scrambling through rocks
– but so far below, almost soundless.

She refused to go through the gate:
I am eighty, you know. But we don't know
– age doesn't happen to us: we see
the slowing down, unsteadiness, the needing
a little sit or a nap, know the dates
and still sense none of it applies to us.
A friend writes from the town where she resettled
Most people leave it too late. I shall: one day
wandering the uncut meadow, not making it back.

If I track my life backwards
through the flukes and chaos and choices
that ended up here, I come to a turn
one early summer evening in my twenties –
when I'd have said you were winding me up
if you'd told me what it would lead to.
I remember that white wool trouser suit
with my lightweight jumper in burnt orange:
they wouldn't last a minute now, here.

Hearthed
for Jonathan Greene

I was young enough to believe in fate.
It was November, the river frozen –
an ice-crust suspended between rocks,
echoes of flow knocking beneath.

The roof had started to slip: one more winter
and it would have been too late, a ruin.
Byres with slate boskins. Old timbers. Centuries
of smells. Two major cracks in one end.

No water. The wartime Farm Survey listed it
on 'roof water'. A hundred yards downhill, once,
a well – a useful hole for the twentieth century's
rubble and rubbish – but a field away

a private pipe, itself off a pipe off
the Haweswater aqueduct. Five owners:
some said lead; others, asbestos. Wrangles,
documents, signatures – one long length of blue alkathene.

No electric. Switch-gear on the nearest 3-phase,
poles, transformers, overheads. (One night
woken by a phone call to say a pole was on fire:
a hill-top beacon with all that creosote.)

No road. A farm track for tractors:
mud, muck, potholes. Milk cows twice a day,
their mournful slobber at the fence
to gaze at what had once been home –

call it fate, call it a calling, intuition,
youth's plain stubborn folly – it no longer matters,
waking each morning to the same views
in some new manifestation: belonging.

Beam

Old. Older than me, you, than anything else
I could show you. And above me
for thousands and thousands of hours

though it was my long slow summer
waiting for a miracle, I came to know
its shifting population, unseen

as a doe holding still in leaf shadow,
for who's here depends on the light
– low sun, ceiling light, reading lamp –

but the woman with thick curly hair's
frequent, Rorschaching to a sharp parting
on a Brylcreemed head above bootlace tie

while a crowd at the far end comes and goes:
a fat sourface, a red nose, a wolf, devil, cat, pig.
Of course I've seen a skull.

I want to say it's been here since
the Second Enclosures Act
holding up a hayloft above boskins,

straight and so hard nails bounce off,
adzed along its length with one rough patch
– that was me, wire-brushing woodworm frass –

but it's had other lives: a nine-inch notch
with two peg-holes, paired notches and a peg-stub
show it once fitted and fixed an elsewhere

though its good length, with only one knot
and its starburst grain, is what points to
a real life of its own before any of this:

a tall and familiar shape against sky
by the drove road – how far back are we now?
that slight warming in the Little Ice Age? –

to give us a trunk thick enough to be felled
then half-sawn – even that, two or three centuries on
from its acorn's white rootlet feeling for soil,

cell upon cell working wonders,
drawing sunlight inside itself into patterns
to look down as faces above this bed.

The houses

Winter evenings, when there were just the two of us
we'd work on another house for the street.
House or bungalow? I liked bungalows best,
their hipped roofs and gables drawn
on card along his scale rule, his Faber Castell
whittled fine and long with his pocket knife – and where
should the doors go, the windows and how many tabs,
and remember the roof needs them too. Then the cutting out
and mystery of how 2D could enfold 3.
Later he'd work on the table at a Bill of Quantities,
column after column, while I painted the houses. That child
seemed to believe in red pantiles and whitewash.
Maybe a memory of my *wanting* but him saying
We can do better ourselves
is a later addition but rings true.

I remember it as pure joy, that work on the hearthrug
in front of the fire. I remember a whole streetful
of houses along a lane that led to a field
with green hedges and black and white cows and one brown
(it's possible the cows were bought in)
though that child must also have been wilful or rude,
for I remember the shocked heartbreak of watching
dear houses thrown on the fireback and though he
helped re-build, even one with leaded lights,
I think the life of that street must have gone up
in the chimney smoke; when I try now to picture his hands
– strong hands with an unbreakable grip – they're
old with stiff-jointed fingers that would pass
over a hearing aid for me to adjust a knob
too fiddly for the likes of me.

The dead never leave II

The dead do not leave. On sleepless nights
they clamber under the covers, board-stiff,
to warm themselves on your memories.

Old, their fingers bent, gait slow and something
hesitant in how they go about the world
– this will not do, they complain:

can you not remember them young and strong,
arms wide for the catch, when they could still laugh,
when they were sure of themselves

and you say it doesn't work like that: the canvas
isn't big enough; memory layers each year
over the past and the paint's only fresh on yesterday

like the too-much-soap-powder-smell of the shirt
on one you loved most who, as always, has the last word:
don't you worry about me; you've a life of your own to get on with.

Shelved

She's nine, wants to run round the whole house.
She stands still for a moment, goes quiet
in front of a wall of shelves then asks
'Have you read all those books?'
I know enough not to reply 'At your age ...'
It's the first time she's stayed here
on her own: we'll sit in bed reading Mole's
riverbank adventures away from home.

You'd think after a lifetime with books,
I'd have a take on the world
that makes sense of it all and what lies ahead.
I wangled 9 library tickets to change
Wednesdays after games and Saturday mornings,
working all the stacks clockwise from the left.
That library was alphabetic. I'd reached
Psychology 150 before I left home.

Maybe it would have come together
if I'd made it to Science 500 or Theology 210;
maybe I'd have some notion of what it's been about
instead of this ragbag of Latin plant names, the average
calf birth-weight on Rum, why no two rainbows
are the same, how Lady Anne Clifford
(dead three hundred years) 'would not have liked it',
electricity in her almshouses,

and that's not to count the two overweight carloads
of statistics and politics and structuralism
I drove off to Clitheroe last year, doubting
any use in their outdated thought,
nor these double-stacked paperbacks,
orange novels with their unremembered plots,

turquoise Pelicans with their cutting edge ideas
mere passage markers for my own decades,

their underlinings and margin scribbles
incomprehensible now, as strange to me as the photo
my young god-daughter finds and asks
'Is that you?' Yes: twenty-three, head
already crammed by those books and so sure of herself
– badly in need of advice I could give myself now
though of course if I'd had it and heeded, I wouldn't
be who I am now and able to give it.

Spine

Then, as if à *propos* of nothing, she asked
whether I remembered the Ice Man
– which I did, though it must have been a while ago,
twenty years? – more than that, she thought:
they'd worked on him for decades, knew his age,
his genes (oddly for the Tyrol, they were Corsican),
how his clothes were made and what he ate
and how he carried tools about his person
as well as fungi used for tinder and for medicine
(he had bad teeth, bad knees and ankles)
but what they didn't know was why he had
a small tattoo just *here* – her finger
pressing on my spine; tell me, she said
tell me when the pain has gone –
those experts had photographs of his body
pinned around the room yet none of them
could fathom why a mark was inked there
until someone's wife brought lunch and asked
what they were staring at: she saw it
instantly, the pressure point, a meridian –
so that 'finely tapered bone awl' in his pouch
wasn't; it was an acupuncture needle, the tattoo
a marker for where someone should insert
its point to relieve longstanding pain,

so never mind his other sixty charcoaled marks,
never mind an arrow killed him,
what I love about the Ice Man tale is
a man about whom everything is known
(that his shoe size was the same as mine,
that he had eaten ibex two hours before he died,
suffered from parasitic worms and lactose intolerance,
had arsenic in his hair from smelting copper

and was ill three times in his last six months) yet
remains so far beyond our grasp he can become
apocryphal, slotting into any story – as in this version
I receive, in which it is a woman who wanders in
with her experience and common sense, solving
years of archaeologists' puzzling, in order
to give the pressure on my spine
the authority of five millennia of practice.

Twenty years after Maurice Riordan 'The Sloe'

The dead never leave III

The dead do not leave. Everywhere, look:
they've strewed so much of themselves around.
That pink-flowered sheet you've just spread
under the hedge to catch clippings, that's theirs.
Your old green jumper which still fits – every
stitch of it was slipped round their fingers.
They gave you that glass when you left home.
A carved wooden trunk, boys' adventure stories
– their clutter so taken for granted, so much a part
of your own everyday, you don't notice it

until it catches you out, appearing from nowhere
like the leather key-case in your car door pocket,
dropped there after you'd locked their house
– cleared and cleaned one last time – and surfacing
only when your car fails its MOT and goes for scrap,
or like the phrase that isn't yours, but theirs and
unremarked until their neighbour tells you, you sound
just like your father. Come across their handwriting
and here they are, their inimitable selves loud and clear
with a copperplate flourish. Let alone their words.

It's called 'Shifting Baseline Syndrome'

There's no photo of the flowers.
I'm three, posed with a group of adults
in plain winter coats from the rationing years
(a Brownie's dog-eared black-and-whites
merely underlining how unreachable
odd snatches of the past you try for).
An outing to pick cowslips. Someone wanted
that most delicate of country wines; would
pull from stems all the hanging flowerheads;
would measure pint after pint of scented petals.

Our stories are always then and now – moths
on night journeys cleared from windscreens
yet now only occasional singlings, headlamp eyes
late at night batting at a kitchen window.
Though what if you'd asked the grandfather
born the year of the last convict ship,
whose only photo's sepia, wouldn't he have rated
your cowslips, orchids, bees, skylarks, cuckoos
as nothing to what he recalled
around the market garden he grew up in?

And the little grand-daughter who finds
a beetle and tells you she knows it's name –
will she, half a century from now, be describing
her soldier beetle to youngsters who can't imagine
its red and black uniform, let alone its march
up plant stems and down on its good works
and will she recount – as if fable –
your own story of murmurations swooping
like a whale, like an elephant, like a teapot,
a jug pouring itself out to roost in the world?

'When a man grows old, he starts to plant trees'

is what my father would recite each year
when I told him it was planting time again –
and certainly that's true of old Arthur:
whenever I've grown more trees than I need,
his daughter will fetch them for planting
high on the moor where they won't struggle
with deer damage, like mine, but with winds.

This year by way of exchange he sent down
three bags of gooseberries, topped and tailed.
No planting here today, nor up there –
curtains opening to the day's fine drizzle and
a few lazy snowflakes that thicken and take over,
the moor already white, ground too frosted for roots
and old Arthur away to a hospital bed in a town

before I've had time to send word he's rich
now they've worked out what a fifty-year-old tree's
worth in dollars – though he'd be having none of that:
a life farming up on the moor, a man knows
that to take, you give. That moment:
hands in dark earth spreading young roots,
a calm. As of a slate wiped clean.

The dead never leave IV

Buried or burned, the dead do not leave
though we did as they asked: tucked them away
in traditional places – or as near as we could, not
near their ancestors' plots but in new rows
in a field off the bypass. We tell them we're sorry,
know that's not quite where they meant.

The dead who told us they wanted to be scattered
on mountain tops, along beaches, from sea cliffs,
or from high bridges over rivers or estuaries
had us gather after long journeys then
thwarted us, hitched to the breeze – that's not
what they'd meant: they'd meant to stay put.

We wrapped in wool those who'd insisted boldly
on soil fertility, buried them in woodland
in the downpour they'd planned would settle them in
but nothing's simple: new plantings run to nettle,
bramble; old woodland clearings between stumps
and rocks are JCB ruts and mud that overtops boots.

And even if – or maybe especially if – you refuse to do
as you were told ('just dump me at the Crem') you too
will find yourself apologising you got it wrong
along with the rest of us: our 'Sorry...' the opening
for their familiar response. We'll still hear them
down the years. Too late now for them to change.

Back then

When they said slow down they couldn't keep up
on a hill, you said it wasn't much of a slope.

When they said they didn't understand how
it could take so long to get ready of a morning;

when they said their hands hurt and did you think
it was because of the knitting and crocheting

and they'd been to three funeral teas
that week so didn't need to cook at home

– oh, all that was years ago. Only now do you hear them.
It wasn't as if they'd been complaining:

what they were talking about was their surprise
at how the body alters so fast and so far,

at how many and routine were its failures
and what odd blessings you'd seize where you could.

They'd wanted you to listen, so you'd rejoice
in whatever you were able for,

set store by every step you took on what you'd know
in the end as a slope that slowed you down.

How else would they have put this
back then, when you were invincible?

Knock knock knockin' on morning's door

Knock Knock who's there? It's the wind,
a westerly, stormed up the valley
like a steam train through the woods
to batter at the walls, barrel round the house –
but pull back the curtains on a monochrome dawn
and all's still. Dead still.

Knock Knock who's there? Not a creak
from a step on the floorboards upstairs, that's for sure.
Harry it was showed me it wasn't the nails
that were loose but the boards sat uneven on beams,
working themselves up and down nail-shafts,
scrawk-scrawk as you walk.

Knock Knock who's there? It's me, Dick Mashiter
died 1732. You and your words, you put a stop
to my rest in peace. I don't hold with how you live godless
here, in my house, don't hold with it one bit
but it's my job now escorting the souls
of all them as die in this place.

Knock Knock who's there? Oh here's Ken
come to borrow my drain rods and flue brush
to clean out the vent pipe for his ex. If I were to tell him,
I'd be safe in the vice of his hold, but I can't
not now (not like when it was mother who died), not now
there's this virus and variant B.1.1.7.

Knock Knock who's there? Jimmy Mac?
Jimmy, you're too soon in your best black coat,
I'm not done yet: there's papers to get and
people to tell – Jimmy, you can't have him yet
I'm keeping the grief to myself, all of it,
all of it mine.

Kock Kn O! It's you my Love! – you, oh,
I was dreaming you died ... And I open my mouth
to tell you all this but the words that come out are about
a fresh pot of tea and needing a cup myself
and you grin, pull a face: *Sorry I'm late*
and a breeze gets going in the bare twigs of the ash.

The dead never leave V

Our dead do not leave; their numbers grow.
They congregate where you'd expect, watch us
go through the ritual motions and rehearse
their own small satisfactions that no flowers yet
have been quite as good as their own. You can hear them:
Fancy having that hymn. And at his age ...

They used to compare numbers. Lockdowns
altered that: cameras for 'remote' attendance
now fixtures high in the centre of buildings.
Is this how it feels to them – both here
and not here – gazing down from mid-ceiling
to notice who's grey now and who's bald,
as people you know and some you don't process in?
Looking down with their eyes, you see how much
smaller is the room than in memory, you see
hands fish pockets for tissues, how no one speaks,
how everyone keeps their head down. The curtains.

Note to self

Listen. Each living thing
has its own allotment.
When it falls from the air
you don't mourn a mayfly.
Stop counting moons.
Forget *sans everything*
– that line's still out there
insidious, doing its harm.
Hokusai inverted it, claiming
as *worthy of notice* not one
of his works before he was 70:
he said old age would be the time
he'd make progress; in his 90's
he'd see more deeply into life;
by 110 every brushstroke of his
would be alive. On his deathbed
(don't quibble about translations)
his last words *If I could have
but one more day...*
are a good place to start.

Topping and tailing blackcurrants at the back window

– the window wide and the evening scent of lilies.
Some small creature struggling along the stones
in the heat, rolls over – a huge beetle? Binoculars:
the drunken creature ducks under the doorstep,
rushes out, rolls again – it's a bee,
a queen *hypnorum*, bright orange thorax doubled
by the matching small male on her back she's
trying everything to throw off.

A dart of air into the climbing hydrangea,
in and out of last year's nest at the speed of invisibility
the moment they return from Africa, and off
just as secretly, must be soon now, in a moonlight flit
– the acrobatics of flycatching! – while the white bowl
fills slowly, so slowly with clean fruit,
a ladybird wandering around in the pile
of stalks and leaves and rejects, and sometimes

the beating of small wings and still the scent of lilies
as if this is how it always is, as if hoverflies
were not having to take over from honey bees,
as if platoons of processionary oak moth
were not already foraging beyond their control zone,
as if plastics were not... as if the week's newspaper cuttings
waiting on the table (and that bee) were not telling how
it is already otherwise.

Redlisted

The last two wingbeats of its three thousand miles:
over the gate and arrowing towards the house,
straight into checking the cobwebs and mosses
of last year's nest in the climbing hydrangea.

Flycatchers are back! Well, one of them is,
though I can't tell them apart and anyway
it could be one of last year's three chicks –
but it knows the patch well, off to the crabapple perch

where I saw one snap a wasp mid-air
to rub out the sting-end on a branch. Is this
where it's at home? or is home where it winters?
or do unbordered skies make them one?

*

From nets over tamarisk trees south of Motole
a small boy untangles a shrike, a flycatcher,
two chiffchaffs, a blackcap, more willow warblers;
his father rips feathers, bags up the meat.

Grandfather counts profits – but these aren't the old ways:
industrial mist-nets, decoy-calls from a mobile.
You'd think we'd know by now how it happens, after
those thirty-mile-long flocks of passenger pigeons

that darkened the sky flying over, hour after hour
and so dense you could shoot with your eyes shut
and bring plenty down – cheap food shipped off
by the trainload – and all gone by the turn of the century

except 'Martha', the very last one in Cincinnati zoo
spinning out her species extinction to 1914.
A life taken here, a habitat there – up goes the price.
And only one flycatcher's back.

Dry

Stalks and a few dead thistles, though
the field not empty after all: sheep
laid out the length of a hedgerow ditch
for what shade they can find. Over
the stile and my own land no better:
dead grass, leafless elder, most hazels
withered and brown, birch shedding
and the stream my geese use
replaced long since by plastic buckets.
Not from this sky, the 60% predicted
rain: cloud too high, too white and
even that skirts low to the south,
some other valley sliding into shade.
Every day, the forecasts' broken promises;
every day, reading the sky upwind
and willing rain to be written there.
Wells are dry. Okay, okay this is not
drought: boreholes still tap
deep groundwater and mere inches
of rain could change dust to verdure –
but it gives imagination something
to work with, to suppose we wait for rains
that don't come this year, that don't come
next, like so many have done already
before setting out for an elsewhere.

Seen when not looking

The first time – struggling with the gate, arms
full of kindling gathered under ash trees down the track –
it was more of an awareness alongside me,
a whiteness swerving into the field, than a sighting.

Then at breakfast, a white underwing flash
had us both run upstairs for the view downhill:
There! There, folded into stillness on a fence post.

The third time was a tea break in the lee of the barn:
she flew round the corner and curved close and low
across the track. We looked at each other, no words.

Later, driving at dusk down the valley, head-on
her gold-and-white blaze in headlights dazzled us, lifted
and vanished – yet it's the presence at the gate

almost unseen, that haunts: that first sense
you daren't count on, though that was the moment
you were pulled out of yourself and held your breath

– as when an unknown dark raptor on the moor
glided below me close to the ground, a shape
imprinted years ago I know now to have been
a harrier. One of the last before they were killed.

Hold out your hand,

I give you a wren –
how many could you hold? three? four?

Ask them raise their beaks and sing:
a chorus so strong – don't drop them –

heads back, song spilling up – they give it all,
every iota of breath to their syrinx – louder

than any song of yours, you with your great lungs
keeping back only the tiniest of airs for your larynx.

Morris Graves painted birdsong in moonlight
as 'white writing', fine white marks

crystallising against darkness – a technique
he'd copied from Mark Tobey's calligraphy –

though whenever I look for that painting
it's never as I remember: his sounds

settle into a cloak of fine gauze,
closer round the bird than I imagine –

your warm handful, see how its song cascades
outwards and up   to fall like rain   like blessing.

The sighting

One glimpse and they were over the roof:
not starlings (they weren't black, close-packed
and disciplined) and not the flock
of great- and coal- and blue-tits that wavers up
most mornings from the Old Wood
(though the mind doesn't work this out in words
but compares instant images of birds arrowing
at 40mph against small birds flitting
every-which-way as if directionless
yet their whole flock's bubble of air
stately to the Little Wood) – these

were fieldfares, their flight loose and inevitable
and I should have called you
because the overcast whiteness of sky
towards Burnmoor resolved into speckles
translating themselves to a wide band of birds,
fairly low – about two hundred feet –
out of the east and over the roof and gone
and still I hadn't called and there were more,
another wave precipitating out of distance
and I was counting, a thousand, two thousand
three... and had I missed the earliest?

It was mid-afternoon and the light
was beginning to alter as the sun hung on
over Cragg Wood. Why tell you this now,
after they've gone? To seal it with words:
mid-November and the wind turned east
and steady, and there were thousands of them
migrating to Ireland. A few years on
and we'll be saying Can you remember?
When was the last time?

We were right underneath their main route
here   and this was the year.

A short cut home

across a neighbour's field – so much to do
and not much time – and over the fence,
forgetting
            that to step into the Little Wood
is to step outside yourself to where time
doesn't measure itself in ticks and hours
but flows through seasons into centuries
and has you tugging fallen willow to find it
not yet light enough for firewood, has you
adding twigs to every brash pile you pass
and – as you always do – checking young trees,
those still in deer-guards, while listening
to the drone, smiling at your foolishness
all those times you'd looked inside wild daffs
instead of 30ft above you at goat willows
to bumblebees in bliss among gold catkins,
though now the *Sarcoscyphus coccinea*,
February's scarlet cups, are gone from moss,
the moss itself a less sharp shade of green,
forgetting too
            how there's always something
to waylay you or surprise – the roebuck
no longer does, leaping up and crashing off
(if he'd lie up, stay still, you'd not notice him) –
this time the way's blocked unaccountably
by a wall of white where you know there's no
bush nor tree, so it takes a while to work out
it's half the crown of an ancient blackthorn, broken
but heavy with sap and still in bud – a while,
because it's thornless, when everyone round here
knows someone with a friend hospitalised
by a blackthorn spine in a swollen thumb,
to be told *Just in time*, any longer and

their arm would have had to come off –
though none of your texts give it so deadly
a character, not even Culpepper, this
whitely blossoming jugful flaring next morning
on the kitchen table in a shaft of sunlight, hundreds
of five-petalled blossoms (except there's a
six-petalled one and some eights, and a ten)
with star-bursts of stamens – which Keble Martin
only illustrates with a smattering of tiny dots –
maybe twenty spraying out from each flower
with minute gold anthers at their tips,
yet not a single one of those poisoned barbs.
And all those jobs you were hurrying home for?
Oh just the usual short term human things,
easy to forget.

Having the luck

Someone
                         looking through my eyes
as I walked along the track through the trees
would have seen fifty yards ahead of us
                     four thin legs
(too thin, they might have thought, to uphold
even that slender body)
                     heedless
among the evening shadows

and when I opened the yard gate, anyone
looking through my eyes
would have seen scribbled on the darkening sky
a circuit above the yard
                     momentarily stall
and dip to take us in –
bats   deer   our commonplace neighbours

so let the expert on small mustelids
stand with me at the kitchen window,
watch this chestnut ribbon of speed
leap, hide, back-flip, play-death,   and
was that really (hard to believe your own eyes)
                     a mid-air corkscrew roll
for – though she's heard *the claims of country people* –
she's never *had the luck,* she writes, *to see*
                     a stoat dancing

I want her to watch this youngster
circling a dead leaf on the grass:
how he somersaults, stares, feints – until the poor leaf
doesn't know which way's up – pounces
                     kills the leaf

disappears into a bush, reappears elsewhere
kills the leaf again   stands white-bibbed on hind legs
to look around –

Here's luck, I'll say: does that look like *gyrations*
provoked by parasitic worms you found
inside museum specimens' skulls
– or a young creature sharpening his skills?
And shouldn't we applaud: all four feet at a time
                        bounce   bounce   bounce   and away
– didn't he look pleased with himself?
Don't anthropomorphise, she can tell me.

Sometimes they recover

The early morning time I love: before full colour,
before the breeze, stirring porridge
– startled by a crack at the window
a not-quite-glimpsed away of white ghost wings
and running outside to find   ah, that song thrush –

all week he'd sung from the top twig of the tallest birch.
He'd started Monday, a few rasps, squawks – newbie
from a tuneless dynasty all racket and repeat –
by Thursday, he'd worked up to a day-long claim on the patch
and already I'd been ill-wishing him though

not this   whimpering   his legs pushing
(and no reason to fly fast at an unlit window unless
rootling on the ground   and that barn owl   curving low?)
silence   falling all around from the tall birch.
Sometimes they recover   but not this

so small, grounded. Such thin pale legs.
And look: more precise than in any bird book,
his breast's black chevrons – and spread coverts
each edged with a matched gold band
you'd never see glint on live wings in flight.

When I came across a dead robin last summer, I tossed it
on the roof where the stoat would climb from the log pile
to feed her kits in the attic – not enough
but it vanished in minutes.
I didn't see who   uplifted the thrush.

yesterday the wind

as if with care
a black wing primary
perfect   on the doormat

sheep's wool and cattle hair
unwoven   near the nest
(a tree rat)

I was in the Old Wood by the river
heard deer bark
heard a sudden wind above the canopy

droplets smacking sycamore leaves
dry under low hazel
thunder

treeshelter to treeshelter
a route home
zigzag and roundabout

today the wind
lays on the doormat
a pearl-grey goose secondary

lays on the meadow's long grasses
a twisted dead medlar branch
I should have pruned long since

Namesake

It took us by surprise, the G.
What with the chainsaw and the beck's
after-rain rampage while we mended
a fence the far side of the gulley,
we heard nothing. It was sheltered anyway
down there: on hazel and alder
catkins hung powdered with pollen.

Only when we carted tools back uphill
did we see the crows' nest at the top of its birch
yawing over and back in wide arcs, every tree
flexing and straining in battering winds –
not the normal low rumble of gusts
storming up the valley and on,
but a high-pitched river of violent air.

My namesake's over the Atlantic
waiting her turn behind Hannah and Idris,
her molecules of water vapour vibrating
to the Iceland low and Azores high, though
no telling yet whether H and I will rush
to follow G, nor whether she'll swell full-term
with cyclogenesis or drift apart –

if she does come, she'll be evil:
out of season to thrash the new-leafed world
beyond what it can bear, the swift rip and shove
of a summer storm flipping aside years
of what seemed solid. It's already March and
we're not often hit by Js, though down the line
we'll be worrying about Tristrams, Violets and Wyns.

September again

Ripped from the tail-end of summer, September's
the fastest month, rushing us to the darkness ahead, sun
down three minutes sooner each day than the one before.
Hard to believe, with this untimely frost, then wind-and-rain,
we'd carry our coffees outside after supper not long since
to sit on the wall, its stones holding the warmth of a sun
well to the north of west. Harder still to account for
where the time's gone between funerals we went to
and those we didn't.
                    Though September
can slam on the brakes and hold its breath, mist
cathedralling morning's yellow light between tree trunks.
Maybe our own last quarters will be lightened by times
of Indian summer as quiet as this – lovely
to think so, as we hurtle towards our own darks –
yet ask anyone round here (as if casually) how they're doing
and they'll tell you they still work hard as they always did,
just these days everything takes that much longer.

Why it's hard to concentrate

Rain. The drifting and clinging kind:
a desk day – but are those fresh molehills
by the field gate? Binoculars reconfigure them
into hares hunched face-to-face,
ears flat-packed, fur sodden and dark,
a wary slit in closed eyes.
Geese nowhere in sight.

I'm watching rain. The desk again.
Check again: still there. Keep checking.
One sits up, shakes and shakes off
a cloud of spray. The second one shakes,
takes a desultory nibble, sits up
on hind legs and washes head, ears;
paddles front feet, works on ears again.

Next time I look, they've gone
but the geese are there preening,
re-arranging every feather just so
as if there's something in the air they've
picked up about readying themselves –
and there is: sky lightens, rain stops
and low out west there's even some blue,

almost bright – and the great white-and-gold
glide of the barn owl cases the fields,
all that energy expended in silent flapping
and cornering round the garden and under trees
though she knows where she's going,
repeating the loops and slight lifts over hedges
– and now the small birds, blackbird on the gate

and the owl again, hungry after a wet night
lands on the grass beside the track,
a couple of bothersome magpies back and forth
between the nearest trees and she's off
to a low branch of ancient ash, breast gleaming,
a steady beacon among the glitter of droplets
on every twig as the sun comes out. And so do I.

Album

An *Acer cappdocium* I grew all those years ago from seed
in ignorance, then, of how much air
                              it would overfill
                                                is always first:
overnight, leaves   clear buttercup
– and always on a morning with the sun behind you
so they blaze
                against a depth of blue.

Second, an old ash tree down the track pales to lime
then almost lemon
                        and   bleaches in late evening light
                                  so it heaves and billows
white
        as if you're seeing in infrared.

Curtains open to dawn-light as if colour
                                          stains the air itself,
field maple beyond the study window hitting
the same yellow note as the carpet
                                          twinning outdoors and in;

berries on the guelder-rose across the field match scarlet leaves;
red-stemmed dogwood's hung with pink and cream;
early morning steps footprint dew as tell-tale as snow

 – moments   are how I think of October, brief
in the manner of photos of things we want to remember
as we look back from the future   forgetting
the dailiness,
                  day after day of rain, dull skies
and dark before you're done
                                the mundane and the tedious uncounted

while at each bend and steep of single track roads to the moor
neat heaps of salt-grit appear
                              in readiness

Thirteenth of December

Sun dipped behind Cragg Hall, as far south as it goes:
229 degrees at 15.48 and that's it –
down a few seconds later tomorrow, swinging
imperceptible minutes back towards west
and its promise of light in late afternoons.

The tawny waits for civil twilight to end.
Most days you'll see him. Today –
just as you're turning away – he swoops down
from the back door of his tree exactly
on time. All else is out of kilter:

yellow blooms on the rose by the bedroom window,
leaves like ripe nectarines on azaleas,
artichokes sprouting fresh offerings regardless,
gnats herky jerky up ladders in their swarm,
snaking down, starting again.

The brand new grey Hilux you didn't recognise
parked on the verge last week drives down
to your neighbour's land. At your desk an hour later
the *phup phup* of silenced shots. Time passes.
The grey pick-up drives out, cargo bed covered.

When you tell Ken he says, *Maybe they missed.*
You've only to look at him and he says, *No;
no, they wouldn't miss.* Twelve days to Christmas
and the season for doe. Looking out from your desk
you could think nothing had happened.

Minus 8 °C

Wool vest, cotton polo, down bodywarmer, fleece jacket
and get the sequence right this time: vest tucked
into leggings, long hand-knitted fisherman's socks next
(one time souvenir become lifesaver) then lined trousers.
To start on the day's lifting and carrying, add
wool hat and scarf, old coat, boots.
Sort out some gloves, though none warm enough.

Unnervingly still, cold air still slices through.
Logs from the pile to the basket. A bucket of feed
down the field for the geese, cans of water
down the field for the geese– ice so thick
in their troughs it can't be kicked in.
Ditches and becks freeze-dried, iced-over river
studded with snow-covered boulders.

Muscles strained from being worked too cold.
Not enough salt-grit for a freeze lasting this long
and how to manage all this when you're old?
Plenty of lessons in this ice –
and for us all – though we'll go on
like Easter Islanders, holding to our faith
in back-to-normal-before-long.

An 'Arctic maritime airmass impact'

Where your boots had tracked through snow,
a dead pheasant: not fox, not badger –
only one side of the breast eaten away,
the killer too small to make off with its kill.
Maybe the feral cat you thought you saw
evaporating into shadow last week.

Next morning an eviscerated bloody mess
dragged a dozen paces off, vivid on snow.
No sign of the head. Late in the day
a pair of crows en route to their roost
paused on the ash crown, parleyed,
dropped down to their undertaking.

Cleared of bright feathers, how tidy they left it:
attached to the bare pink beads of a spine
pale leg bones dangled scaly grey claws
at ungainly angles – like legs which had danced
and clattered on stage before their puppeteer
had laid them and their act aside.

As snow melted, the feathers spread –
small creatures cleaning off even the skin
that had held them before worms seize each shaft
to tug down into earth. The legs lay
as if waiting for tomorrow's performance
but their next act – like the snow's – was to vanish.

Second of January

Daybreak: the purpledark loosing its grip
with a trace of almost green at the skyline;
crimson underbellies on far-off small clouds then
the full ripe-fruit colour scheme through to oranges
and the gold horizon seeming to burn
where you think the sun will rise – wrong:
the brightness slides on southwards until
the air itself over Raven's Castle is on fire
and your eyes can't take the sunburst
                                          and you get to thinking
this is as late as it rises, as far south as it goes
and wonder how long it will be, surfacing each day
further north now, before the flare of a sunrise
crowns Ingleborough. Midsummer?   Mid-thought
you catch yourself – that's not how it works –
try instead to feel this home sphere rolling east,
you and the birch trees you're standing under,
the air you're breathing, the creamy clouds,
all of us in a six-hundred-mile-an-hour hurtle
east into the light then down into winterdark
with the ground starting its slight tilt southwards
so next time around the sun will reach higher
than this 13 degrees slip across the horizon
drawing its longest shadows across the snow
– and for a moment   you think you get it
                                          but can't hold it:
your earthbound feet, the still and steadfast trees
your primitive senses fixing you   here   now
                                          though you forgot
that's nothing to our annual hundred-times-faster
trip around the sun – the noise of that
                                          if you could hear

The last resort

For a while it worked, ordering life's small essentials,
the grey plastic tray an almost perfect fit for your desk drawer:
compartments for paper clips, pencil leads, labels, stamps,
then picture hooks with pins, bolts and washers, keys
that might fit suitcases, even a space at the back for childhood's
silver sixpences from Christmas puddings and a ten cent piece
in currency with a brigantine in full sail on its reverse –

though it evolved into a magnet for things with nowhere else to go,
for what might come in (a tiny filament bulb, though all
your torches now are LEDs) or useless things with histories
still attached (your last spent cartridge) or others you couldn't
bring yourself to throw away (the seed packet from Vladivostock
hand-written in Cyrillic script) and always now the place of last resort
when a half-inch crosshead screw you know is just to hand is not

so when you're desperate for a drawing pin today which must
be somewhere among the fluff and dirt, you're rummaging history,
except you forget what it was you were looking for
when a rusted black lapel badge draws attention to itself,
its sharp white lines semaphoring N and D and freighted
with those long forgotten fears from fifty years ago.
You remember how that felt. History: you pin it on.

Without which

not the big cats, those stylish loners,
not (cue slow strings – when the soundtrack
should be wind – or silence) a last polar bear,
not quirky frogs or white saddle fungus,
not creatures of flock and colony and herd
who know how life depends on others, not
all the glorious tree forms we're outlived by,
not the prettiest like Peacocks, Painted Ladies,
Red Admirals and the rest, not the most fragrant
(my *Gruss an Aachen* rose, my fresh-picked
Sunset apple) nor the tastiest (that apple again),
the oldest, the most bizarre, the least understood,
not even the rare white harebell I found
on a bank, telling no one its whereabouts –

but this busy world of exchange and engineering
my friend from Vermont persists in calling *dirt*,
the billions of untold lives I'm cradling
in this handful of warm dark earth that smells
of the past and of this moment and just here
and of which one day I too will be a part

Which way up to chit a potato?

Breakfast talk sets off from the broken daffodil bud
propped in a milk bottle for me to identify
in case it'll be the (rare now) February Silver
I'd thought lost to narcissus blight, but diverts
by way of genetic modifications to leapfrog
the garden fence for why wild daffs in the wood
might be immune and spread too densely there
but could thin out as soil depletes, then sidesteps
to how foxgloves are a pest in the vegetable beds
yet never show at the woods' edges which
must be about disturbance, since whenever
you lay a hedge, the next year it's foxgloves
all along in that sudden access of light:

all the things you didn't know you knew
– picked up on a great uncle's allotment or
handed down with rare plants by an elderly friend
when arthritis kept her housebound –
grounding a lifetime of reading, to surface again
when you're asked why not or what for,
so much you didn't know you knew:
All that stuff you've got in your head! which is rich
coming from him, a man who'll tell me the make
of a tractor grumbling uphill quarter of a mile off,
who can dismantle and sort anything metal and
– eyes closed – will feel for what he calls
the sweet spot and when found shouts *YES!*

though I know what he means: I still remember
my surprise years ago when an old friend
who'd spent his life tending sick children, told me
it won't be too long before far more than we expect
turns out to be carried in our genes –

which always left me wondering where
it came from, my own feeling for that *YES*,
the moment when a hull and the sails and the waves
and the wind concur with a flow that's neither
been learned nor explained, but is something
I know in my bones, as if natural
for someone whose great-grandfather built boats
(though, of course, another grew trees).

Walking Around III

No wind. A wasp circling close – the wood's only sound.
Spillages of sun soak into the grey-brown drugget
of last year's leaves. Time   passes.
A tiny bronze beetle motors round my cuff.

Trunks are slender and tall – a young wood
on old woodland floor, clear-felled a few decades back
to the odd straggled birch and left, unfenced,
to its own devices and re-growth:

nurse trees were fast, hazel and rowan
and more birch; now oak and beech fill in.
I hear a car pass on the road and like the idea
no one knows I'm here, out of time, out of life.

Walking on, my pulse is slow. You could say it's
the air in the wood, easy oxygen and dust-free or
you could say time cycles differently here,
lifetimes measured in seasons and centuries.

Fewer ferns on a track through dense growth,
a beech badly deer-frayed, a curve east
and hazels hang low – I duck and should know I'm
where I always walk at the top of the wood, out

into brightness that invariably startles
– far hills like sphinxes on guard at the horizon –
this shock of being delivered back into the world
and full of slow woodliness.

Malus sylvestris, *60-90 cm, January 2022*

Little tree, I should have kept a ledger.
I can't give you an exact age for your new companions;
most are quite young, about twenty and – sheltered
by hedgerow and holly – tall for their age.

Here is your space: there's some shade from birch,
alder and birdcherry and a thicket of guelder;
here are fungi for your roots, a mat of leaves and moss
to smother weeds and rot down.

You'll need this guard against deer fraying your bark
and grazing your growth; this stake
to help brace you against northerlies
until you've your own fast hold on the ground.

Little one, grow well. I'll not see you crowned and crabbed
nor your ploys to spread seed, though this planting
will be recorded in your roots and your rings;
I do what I can before the time that is coming.

Tree correspondence (NZ)

Dear A, Great your protest saved the old totaras!
I thought of you that day – your midwinter
likely warmer than our midsummer's day –
no idea you'd have (even with a hoist)
so many willing to climb and stay put.

You ask about the plantings here, ash die-back.
Young trees you saw in deer-guards are now
tall and stately beings – their own selves
living lives beyond any plans of mine.
They give land back some mystery and depth.

Roadside veterans I'd thought I'd have to fell
leafed up, late of course in breaking out
from epicorms, but strong enough this season
unless there's re-infection. There's little yet:
what few black drooping leaves I've found, I burned.

I'm often asked advice these days for die-back
(those early years' *nothing but a field of sticks*
or *good grazing gone to waste* forgotten
in the face of 60-footers). 'Wait' I say
though that answer's not what's wanted.

We're so short-term; affected trees
aren't *ugly*, they're miraculous:
diseased wood sealed off, fresh growth begun.
And even if trees die, standing deadwood
houses far more species than does líve –

you know all this. Coincidence to find
like you, I'm trying to thwart the saws –
and how glad I've been of trees these last hot weeks,
walking out early into cool, clean air
easy to breathe and soothing on the skin,

grasses along the wood-edge shoulder high,
their spires and feathers and bottlebrushes
caught by low morning sun before the breeze
as if cast in silver. Uncountable blessings.
Uncountable losses to come. Yours, J.

The Old Wood

For all that new plantings can sometimes feel
like a playgroundful of youngsters to keep an eye on,
attention always needed by the weak or fallen

and though three birches, grown from seed germinated
the month my god-daughter was born, then planted out
two fields away, are now – like her – full height

and while the ancient alder by the gate, stout and gnarled
and shedding branches as it slowly dies, brings to mind
a grumpy neighbour taking note of all your ins and outs

and despite the ash tree by the kitchen window almost being
family – always with us at the table through whatever
winds and weathers, the Old Wood above the river

is itself. Rustles and creaks are all that break its silence.
The pack road to the ford's long gone: outgrown coppice
the only sign the wood was worked for centuries,

its foot- and hand-holds unstable now among leaning trunks,
gulleys, cliffs and landslips. Unpeopled, rank, the Old Wood's wild:
degenerate, rotting – free of human neediness.

It's a mast year again

and the oaks of course are bigger than last time so there are more
acorns are everywhere underfoot like skating on ball-bearings

rooks are flying off with them squirrels are hoarding them mice
fatten and jays stab them down into the lawn and check sightlines

some already anchored upright their fat white rootlets
reaching for good earth to tow the nut down into dark safety

I ask you help sweep up the leaves and you bring me
a washing-up bowl full of acorns where do I want them

not in the compost not in the leaf bin why not back under an oak
close in by the trunk where deep shade will stop a plague of seedlings

but you take them down the field scatter optimism with them
that they'll get away protected by brambles and gorse

and I rake the leaves lightly dull greens and yellows from the ash
grey brown from the oak leaving the shiny bright nuts on the ground

picking out twigs one ash with a blackened leaf and leaf stem
nothing dry about it nothing seasonal about disease   that one I burn

Idle talk,

            that's all it was, my saying
into the evening's fireside silence 'Wouldn't it
be lovely to be able to do it all again – yet
knowing everything you know now?'
My mind had been wandering through the woods,
the cleared bramble patch, the hornbeams to plant

and how much better a start they'll have
than my first plantings did, before I knew
how many deer there are, the damage they do,
before I could guess at a tree's upthrust and spread
and all its attendant alterations to light and air,
to drainage and woodland floor.

You didn't reply for a while. A log shifted
in the fire; a yellow flare. When you did,
it was to ask what it was I'd want to be different
– but all I could say to you was 'Nothing'. There's nothing
I'd want any different from this: red-berried guelder
I planted, ever-flowering gorse that I didn't,

the old woods and new going their own ways now –
so I can laugh about starting back then with sketch-plans
and lists, to find land working on its own terms, not ours
but generously: daily unfolding some new joy
for short-lived creatures like us to uncover
with our idle thoughts and a fireside to think them by.

Notes

'Viruses'
H5N1 caused the 2007 Avian Influenza infections. The UK was hit badly in 2001 by the FMDV type 0 pan Asia mutation of the animal foot and mouth virus. SARS-CoV-2 is the virus causing the disease Covid-19.

'Hearthed'
responds to Jonathan Greene's 'Forethoughts, Buying a Farm'.

'Topping and tailing blackcurrants at the back window'
Bombus hypnorum first arrived in UK from Europe in 2001 and is now widespread.

'Hold out your hand'
Morris Graves: 'Bird singing in the Moonlight', 1938-9 (MoMA)

'The last resort'
Gerald Holtom designed the CND/peace symbol in 1958 for the first Aldermaston march, combining the semaphore signals for N and D.

'When a man grows old he starts to plant trees'
Prof.T.M.Das, University of Calcutta (in *Indian Biologist* 1979) was the first to propose the value of 'environmental benefits and services derived from a tree with an average lifespan of 50 years' could be $196,250.

'Namesake'
Storm names are from the 2018-2019 alphabetical list prepared by Met Éireann and the Met Office.

Acknowledgements

For giving some of these poems their first publication, thanks are due to the editors of *Artemis, International Times, Pennine Platform, Poetry Salzburg, Stride, The Friday Poem, The Frogmore Papers, The High Window, The North, Write where we are now; Live Canon Anthology 2023*. 'The February Museum' won the 2022 Second Light Competition.

Let the grasses remain.
Let the harebell on the bank.
And the quiet community of trees
that showed us how, though we did not heed.

Let skydancers return to the moor.
I like to think of geese in autumn
eating seedheads to prepare for winter ahead –
but all creatures are innocent; ours is the fault.